What's that Building?

Written by Richard Platt
Illustrated by Pulsar Studio

Contents

Collins

What's that building?

How big is a building?
What shape is it?
What's it for?
There's no one answer.
Some buildings are huge
boxes made of glass, some
are long, low and flat,
and others are made of
unusual materials.
Some buildings are
very odd indeed.

This skyscraper's in Taipei,
Taiwan. The strong steel
frame that holds up this
building is hidden inside.

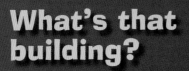

Some buildings are so vast that workers use scooters to get around.

This round stone fort is a Martello tower. It was built with a thick stone wall, to protect it from cannon fire.

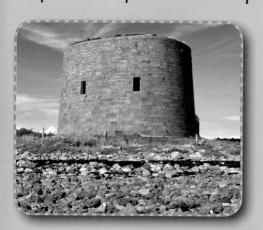

Let's go and see some of the world's most interesting buildings ...

Odd shapes for odd jobs

Aircraft hangar

This building's much taller than it looks from far away.

It's a garage for giant aircraft.

Vast doors keep the cold or heat out while work is done on the planes inside.

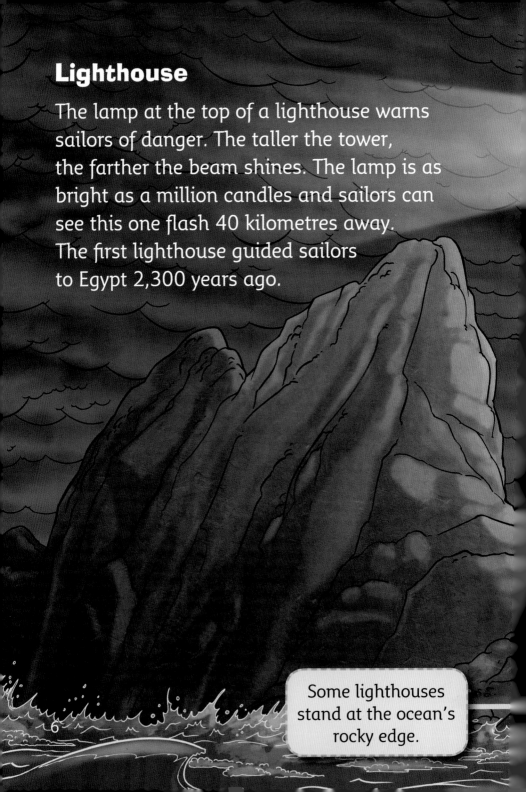

Lighthouse

The lamp at the top of a lighthouse warns sailors of danger. The taller the tower, the farther the beam shines. The lamp is as bright as a million candles and sailors can see this one flash 40 kilometres away. The first lighthouse guided sailors to Egypt 2,300 years ago.

Some lighthouses stand at the ocean's rocky edge.

Palm house

The palm house at Kew Gardens in London, UK, is one big greenhouse. It's the most famous glasshouse at Kew Gardens. Its glass walls trap the sun's rays, to warm the jungle trees growing inside.

The world's oldest potted palm, brought to Kew in 1775, grows here.

Curved iron beams hold up the glass. Their strength allowed the builder to make the palm house wide enough to fill it with the biggest plants.

The 700 panes of glass in this palm house were each curved by hand, one by one.

9

Storing and making things

Water tower

You can't eat this monster mushroom – it's made of concrete. The wide cap is a water store. Pipes spread from the base to buildings nearby. Water flows down the pipes, pushed along by the weight of water stored at the top. Pumps can do the job of a water tower, but they don't work when the power fails.

There's enough water in the tower to fill 11,000 baths!

All water towers are tall, but they have many different shapes. The "concrete mushroom" shape is cheap and easy to build.

Oil rig

Vast oil rigs are made of steel and concrete and are the biggest movable structures in the world. Workers build the rigs on land in several huge pieces. Then they tow them into position in the sea before fixing them together. They rest on the ocean floor, or float in the oceans. Their crews drill holes in the seabed to find oil. Then the rig pumps the oil down pipes to the shore.

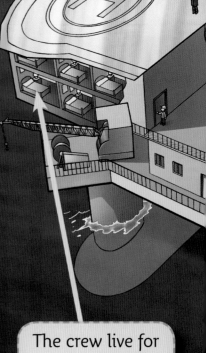

On land, an oil rig would stand as high as a 120-floor building!

The crew live for weeks in these hotel blocks.

The crew arrives by helicopter.

Pumping mud down new wells stops oil squirting out.

Windmill

When is a building a machine, too?
When it's a windmill!
These wooden towers
once ground grain
into flour. Their sails
caught every gust of wind,
turning huge grindstones inside.
People began using electric motors
instead of windmills to make flour
about 100 years ago.

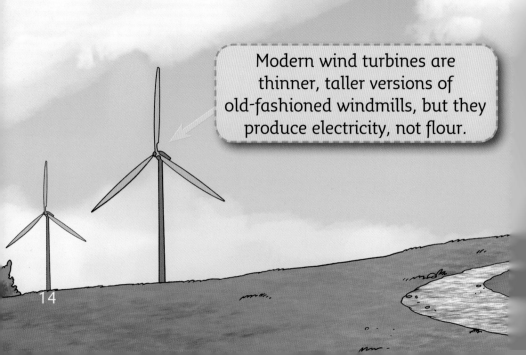

Modern wind turbines are thinner, taller versions of old-fashioned windmills, but they produce electricity, not flour.

Wooden gears turn the shaft that spins the grindstones.

The grindstones crush grain between them as the top one turns.

Pushing this pole turns the mill to face the wind.

15

Buildings for protection

Khufu's pyramid

This stone pyramid rises from the desert near Cairo, Egypt. King Khufu ordered his people to build the pyramid as a massive gravestone for him 4,500 years ago. The work would have kept 100,000 Egyptians busy for up to 20 years. Tourists have been visiting Khufu's pyramid for amore than 2,000 years.

Workers cut over two million blocks of limestone to make the pyramid. Some blocks are bigger than a car.

Building workers used only hand tools, and dragged blocks on sledges!

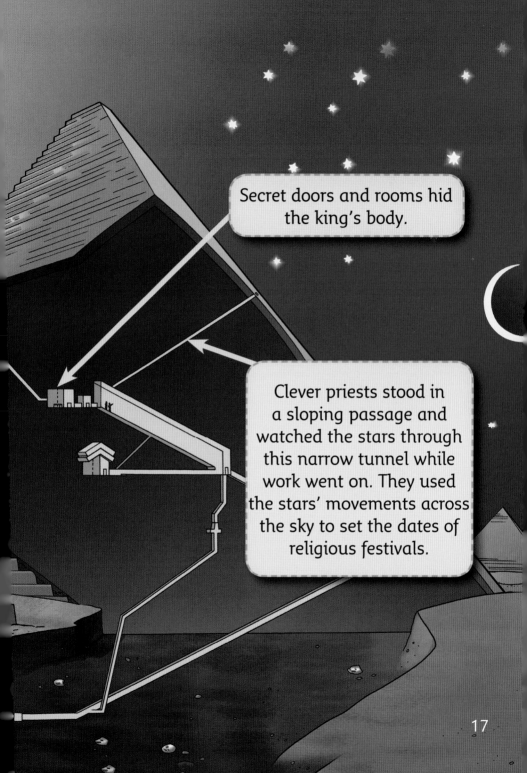

Secret doors and rooms hid the king's body.

Clever priests stood in a sloping passage and watched the stars through this narrow tunnel while work went on. They used the stars' movements across the sky to set the dates of religious festivals.

Nuclear bunker

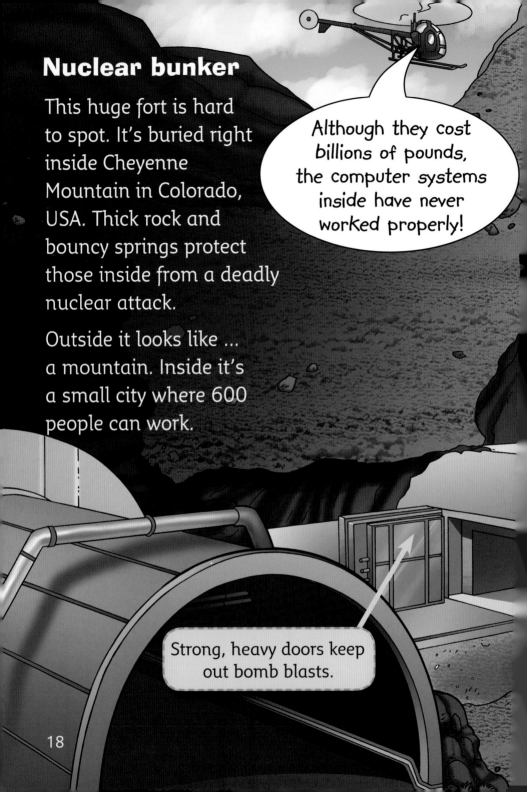

This huge fort is hard to spot. It's buried right inside Cheyenne Mountain in Colorado, USA. Thick rock and bouncy springs protect those inside from a deadly nuclear attack.

Outside it looks like ... a mountain. Inside it's a small city where 600 people can work.

Although they cost billions of pounds, the computer systems inside have never worked properly!

Strong, heavy doors keep out bomb blasts.

If danger threatens, army commanders can seal the fort and live inside with other important people who run the country. People can live inside here for a long time.

19

Timbuktu mosque

One of the world's greatest temples is made of mud.
It's a mosque in Timbuktu, Mali. This city stands
in Africa's scorching Sahara desert.
The old mosque is cleverly built.
Its thick walls shade
the people inside.

The mosque gets
a smart new coat
of mud every year.

The mosque has no
windows so it stays cool
even when it's very hot
outside.

21

What do these buildings do?

make

store